796
HAR

Harvey, Miles.

Italy

DATE DUE

D1443730

games people play!

Italy

Miles Harvey

CHILDREN'S PRESS®
A Division of Grolier Publishing
New York • London • Hong Kong • Sydney
Danbury, Connecticut

Design Staff

Design and Electronic Composition:
 TJS Design

Maps: TJS Design

Cover Art and Icons: Susan Kwas

Activity Page Art: MacArt Design

Library of Congress Cataloging-in-Publication Data

Harvey, Miles.
Italy / by Miles Harvey.
 p. cm. — (Games people play)
Includes bibliographical references and index.
Summary: Surveys the sports and games played in Italy,
from ancient Rome on, with an emphasis on the present day.
ISBN 0-516-20033-X
1. Sports—Italy—History—Juvenile literature. 2. Games—Italy.
[1. Sports—Italy. 2. Games—Italy.] I. Title. II. Series.

GV615.H37 1996   96-31127
796'.0945—dc20   CIP
                                       AC

Table of Contents

4   Meet the *Tifosi*

8   Italy at a Glance

10   Sports in Ancient Rome

18   Soccer

28   Off to the Races

44   Other Competitive Sports

52   Italian Games and Other Leisure Activities

60   Glossary

62   For Further Information

63   Index

Introduction

Meet the *Tifosi*

In Italy, people use an unusual word to describe sports fans. Italian fans are known as *tifosi*, a word that means "those who are infected with typhus."

Typhus is a very serious and contagious illness, meaning that it is passed from one person to another. And in Italy, the love of sports is also contagious. Italians are considered to be some of the most intense and passionate sports fans on earth. Soccer, for instance, is the most popular sport in Italy. If the Italian national soccer team wins when it travels to other countries, the returning players are greeted at the airport by thousands of cheering fans. But if the team does poorly, those same players might be met at the airport by crowds of angry people who jeer and throw rotten vegetables.

Forza Italia

A soccer slogan meaning "Go, Italy!"

Italian prime minister Silvio Berlusconi

This intense emotional attachment to sports affects many aspects of Italian life. In 1994, for example, a man named Silvio Berlusconi ran for prime minister, the top governmental office in Italy. He came up with an interesting name for his political party. Instead of giving it a typical title — such as the Republican Party or the Democratic Party — he named it *Forza Italia,* which is a soccer slogan that means "Go, Italy!" Berlusconi thought that associating himself with soccer would help him win votes — and he was right! After he was elected prime minister, he named the group of politicians who advised him the *Azzurri.* That's the name of the Italian national soccer team.

In the last 100 years or so, millions of Italians have moved to the United States. These Italian-Americans have played a vital role in the American sports scene. For instance, many of baseball's best players, such as Hall of Famer Joe DiMaggio (whose real name is Giuseppe Paolo DiMaggio), were of Italian descent. So were many football greats, such as the legendary coach Vince Lombardi. The same is true for boxing, basketball, hockey, auto racing, and many other sports. But in addition to supplying the United States with some of its best athletes and coaches, Italian-Americans have brought their unique love of sports to American culture. And now, all American sports fans have a little bit of the tifosi in them!

Many Italian-Americans have become sports heroes, including Joe DiMaggio (left), a baseball superstar in the 1940s, and Vince Lombardi (below), the legendary coach of the Green Bay Packers in the 1960s.

Italy at a Glance

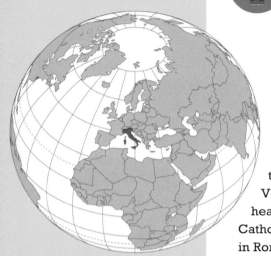

The People

About 58 million people live in Italy. They speak Italian, and most of them are Catholics. The Vatican — the worldwide headquarters of the Roman Catholic Church — is located in Rome, Italy.

The Land

Italy is a long, narrow country that juts down into the Mediterranean Sea in southern Europe. It covers 116,303 square miles (301,270 square kilometers) — about the combined size of the states of Georgia and Florida. Italy's capital is Rome.

Government

The Italian system of government is known as a parliamentary democracy. In this system, the head of government (the prime minister) is elected by Parliament, the national law-making body. The members of Parliament are elected by the citizens.

History

Beginning around 500 B.C., Italy was the center of the Roman Empire, one of the most powerful lands in the ancient world. Ancient Rome collapsed in the fifth century A.D. During the Middle Ages, Italy was ruled by several different foreign invaders. In the 11th century, many Italian cities formed their own independent governments, known as city-states. Beginning in the 14th century, the vibrant cultural life in some of these city-states gave rise to an era of artistic and scientific excellence known as the Italian Renaissance. Starting late in the 15th century, Italy fell victim to invasion and rule by France, Spain, and Austria. In 1861, Italy became an independent kingdom. From 1922 until 1943, Benito Mussolini was dictator of Italy. Since 1946, Italy has been a democracy.

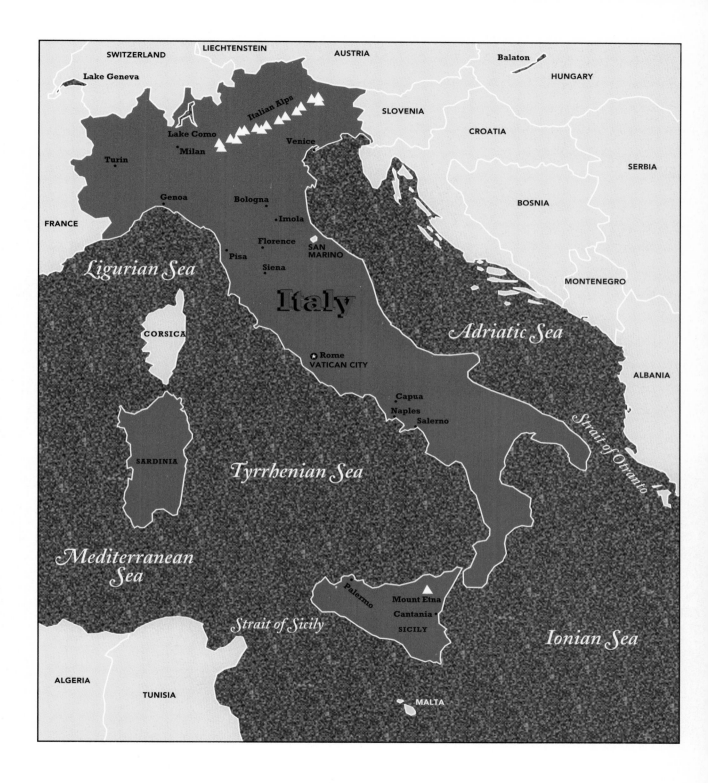

SWITZERLAND
LIECHTENSTEIN
AUSTRIA
Balaton
HUNGARY
Lake Geneva
Italian Alps
SLOVENIA
CROATIA
SERBIA
Lake Como
Venice
Turin
Milan
BOSNIA
Genoa
Bologna
Imola
FRANCE
Florence
Pisa
SAN MARINO
Ligurian Sea
Siena
MONTENEGRO
Italy
Adriatic Sea
CORSICA
Rome
VATICAN CITY
ALBANIA
Capua
Naples
Salerno
SARDINIA
Strait of Otranto
Tyrrhenian Sea
Mediterranean Sea
Palermo
Mount Etna
Cantania
SICILY
Ionian Sea
Strait of Sicily
ALGERIA
TUNISIA
MALTA

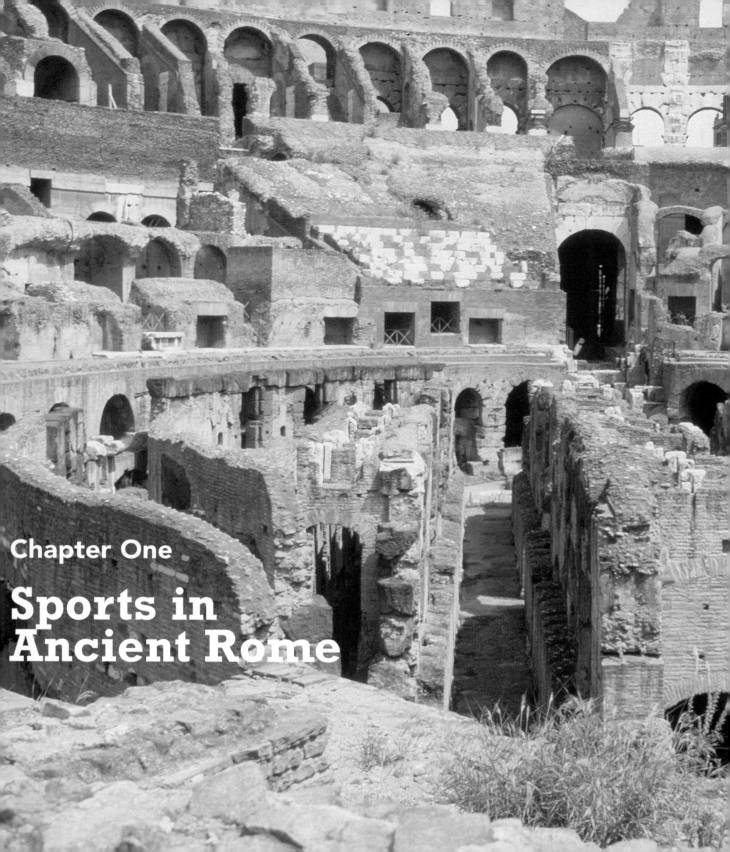

Chapter One

Sports in Ancient Rome

In ancient times, Italy was at the center of a huge and powerful land known as the Roman Empire. This civilization came to an end more than 1,500 years ago — but even today, Roman culture continues to influence our lives.

For example, some of our literature and architecture, as well as parts of our legal and political systems, originally came from ancient Rome. The ancient Romans also passed down to us a love for sports.

According to legend, Rome was founded in 753 B.C. by a man named Romulus and his twin brother, Remus. Shortly after he established Rome, Romulus is said to have held **chariot races**. As Rome grew from a small city to the capital of a huge land that included much of Europe and parts of Asia and Africa, chariot races became incredibly popular.

Above: Chariot races in ancient Rome

Opposite Page: Remains of the Roman Colosseum, where many athletic events took place

11

Chariot races at Circus Maximus

In cities across the Roman Empire, huge stadiums were built for the races. The biggest of these stadiums, named Circus Maximus, was located in the city of Rome. Historians think Circus Maximus could hold as many as 250,000 spectators. That's more than twice as many fans as could fit in the Michigan Football Stadium, the biggest U.S. football stadium.

The chariot was a cart that could be pulled very quickly by galloping horses. Chariot drivers were known as charioteers. In ancient Rome, charioteers were divided into four teams: the Reds, the Whites, the Blues, and the Greens. Just like today, sports fans in ancient Rome had a favorite team. During ancient chariot races, fans of the different teams went wild as they cheered on their favorites.

charioteers

chariot drivers in ancient Rome

12

The racetrack itself was a long oval. In each race, the charioteers went around the oval seven times, a total distance of just over 5 miles (8 kilometers). A race lasted about 15 minutes. There were sometimes as many as 24 races held each day. When the action got very rough, chariots would tip over and drivers were sometimes trampled by the horses. But for Roman fans, this only added to the excitement.

Just like today, lots of kids in ancient Rome dreamed of growing up to become famous athletes. One boy who wanted to become a chariot racer was Nero Claudius Caesar. Nero was a big fan of the Greens, and he loved to play a board game that involved miniature chariot racers. He hoped that one day he would be able to be a great charioteer himself.

Before he could attain that dream, however, Nero became emperor of Rome — at the age of 17. An emperor is pretty much the same thing as a king. He can do whatever he likes, and Nero wanted to be a charioteer. He spent hours practicing on a real chariot and real horses. There was only one problem — he wasn't very good at it. The men who were teaching Nero how to drive the chariot knew he was not skillful enough to be a good racer. But they did not have the courage to tell him.

Emperor Nero

Nero participated in some of the races at Circus Maximus, but he mostly wanted to win in the Olympic Games. In these games, the best athletes in the world gathered every four years in the land of Greece to compete in a variety of different sports. Our modern Olympic Games are based on this ancient festival.

At the Olympic Games of A.D. 67, Nero participated in a very difficult kind of chariot race. Each driver had ten horses pulling his chariot. Controlling that many animals was extremely difficult — especially for a bad driver like Nero. He fell out of his chariot early in the competition. But that didn't mean that Nero had lost. The judges didn't want to make him angry, so

Emperor Nero rides to victory in a chariot race.

they declared Nero the winner — even though he never finished the race!

Another type of sport that was very popular among fans in ancient Rome was the gladiator games. In the modern world, gladiator games would be condemned because they were such a cruel and bloody spectacle. It involved men known as gladiators, who fought each other in front of thousands of cheering spectators. The gladiators used dangerous weapons, such as swords, daggers, and spears. They often battled until one contestant died. A similar Roman sport involved men who fought against wild animals.

In the violent and vicious gladiator games, men fought each other (or animals) to the death.

15

The gladiator games took place in arenas called amphitheaters. In the city of Rome, the biggest of these arenas was the Colosseum. It held 50,000 spectators. Many of our modern sports stadiums resemble the Colosseum and other amphitheaters. The gladiator games faded with the end of the Roman Empire in the fifth century A.D.

Not many people in ancient Rome wanted to be gladiators. That was because the job often ended in serious injury or death. As a result, many slaves, prisoners of war, and criminals were forced to become gladiators.

In present-day Rome, remains of the Colosseum are a major tourist attraction.

Gladiators went to special schools, where they were taught how to use different kinds of weapons and how to perform different types of combat. At some of the schools, the gladiators were treated well. They ate good food and received high-quality medical treatment. But at other schools, they were treated like prisoners. One school that apparently treated its gladiators very badly was in Capua, a city near Naples in what is now southwestern Italy. In the year 73 B.C., many of the gladiators at the Capua school attacked their guards and escaped. These men were led by a gladiator named Spartacus. After their escape, Spartacus and the others went to Mount Vesuvius, a huge volcano that was located near their school. They hid in the crater of the volcano. Luckily for them, it was not shooting out any hot lava at the time!

Soon, many other slaves began to escape from their masters to join Spartacus and his followers. The army tried to capture them, but Spartacus and the other gladiators fought the soldiers off. As the months went on, more and more people began to take sides with Spartacus. As many as 90,000 people eventually joined the escaped gladiators.

Spartacus

a famous gladiator who led a revolt against the Roman government

The conflict between Spartacus and the Roman government quickly grew into war. In 71 B.C., the Roman army finally triumphed. Spartacus was killed, along with many of his followers. But even today, the conflict known as "The Gladiators' War" is still remembered as one of the most important events in the history of ancient Rome.

A gladiator battles a lion.

17

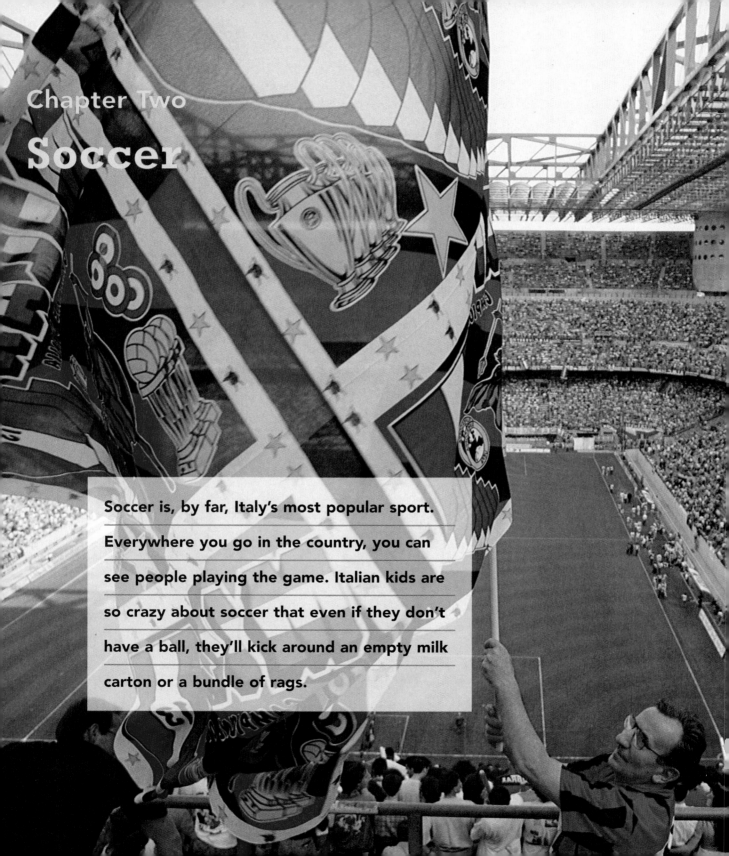

Chapter Two

Soccer

Soccer is, by far, Italy's most popular sport. Everywhere you go in the country, you can see people playing the game. Italian kids are so crazy about soccer that even if they don't have a ball, they'll kick around an empty milk carton or a bundle of rags.

The history of **soccer** (commonly called "football" in most of the world) is long and complex. Historians are not entirely certain how the sport developed through the centuries, but historians believe that more than 3,500 years ago, people in China played a sport that resembled soccer. The ancient Romans also had a ball game involving the feet. It was called *harpastum*. Historians believe that Roman soldiers took this game with them when they conquered England. There, harpastum was combined with English ball games — and the mix of these two games eventually became soccer as we know it today.

Although the English are generally given credit for creating modern soccer, some Italians claim that the game was actually invented in their country. They point out that in the 16th century, people in the city of Florence played a game with teams of more than 20 players on each side. The rules of this game were similar to modern soccer, except that contestants could carry and throw the ball with their hands.

A modern Italian *calcio* festival in which an ancient game similar to soccer is recreated.

Nonetheless, soccer did not gain widespread popularity in Italy until sailors from England arrived there in the late 1880s. When these sailors went ashore in seaports such as Genoa, Leghorn, and Naples, they would take their soccer balls along. Italians saw the British seamen playing, and a few of them began to get interested in the sport.

In 1897, the residents of Turin formed their own soccer team. They called the team the Juventus Football Club. Juventus still exists today, and it is one of the most popular and successful teams in Italy. Around the beginning of the 20th century, other soccer teams began to form all over Italy. These teams joined together in their own soccer league.

In 1910, the first national Italian soccer team was formed. Over the years, the national team has become wildly popular among Italians. Because the team wears blue uniforms, it is known as the Azzurri, which means "the Blues."

In 1930, the first World Cup competition was held. The World Cup is the major international tournament that takes place every four years to determine which country has the best soccer team. Dozens of countries enter their national teams in a series of preliminary rounds that lasts two years to decide the best 24 teams. These countries then qualify for the final rounds, which take place in a specific host country over a three-week period. In 1994, the United States hosted the World Cup final rounds, and in 1998, France will be the host country. The final rounds of the World Cup comprise one of the most exciting and popular sports events in the world.

The Italian national team is called the Azzurri, which is Italian for "the Blues."

The Italian team, which is composed of the best players of all teams in Italy's soccer leagues, did not take part in the first World Cup. But in 1934, the tournament was held in Italy. Playing before supportive home crowds, the Azzurri won the tournament, beating Czechoslovakia 2–1 in the final game. The star of the team was Giuseppe Meazza, who was known for his astonishing ability to pass the ball. Four years later, at the World Cup in France, the Italians won again. In the semifinal game against Brazil, Meazza scored the winning goal. Then, in the championship game against Hungary, he led his team to a 4–2 victory.

In the 1930s, Italy dominated World Cup soccer.

From 1922 until 1943, Italy was ruled by dictator Benito Mussolini, who imposed a system of government on Italy called Fascism, in which individuals have few rights and there is no real democracy. Fascism also had a big impact on Italian soccer. Mussolini went to great lengths to make sure that Italy had the best soccer team in the world. The Fascists built new soccer stadiums

Benito Mussolini (below) believed that physical fitness in a country's leaders and its citizens helped make for a strong and dominant country. During World War II, Mussolini and German dictator Adolf Hitler (left) nearly conquered Europe before being defeated by the Allied nations, including Great Britain and the United States.

all over Italy and also started programs aimed at getting more Italians interested in soccer. Mussolini believed that having a great soccer team would give Italians great pride in their country and make them feel superior to people in other countries.

In 1934, Mussolini convinced organizers of the World Cup to hold the event in Italy. He planned to use the games to show off his country and his fascist system of government. Italy did win the tournament, but the Italian team played with a dirty, violent style that left several players from other teams injured. After the games were over, many people outside of Italy had a worse opinion of Italian Fascism, not a better one. So in a way, Mussolini's plan had backfired.

After several lean decades, Italy returned to dominate international soccer in the 1970s.

Because of World War II (1939–45), the World Cup did not take place until 1950. By this time, the Italian team's best players had retired, and Italian soccer entered a rare low period. The Azzurri didn't make it into a championship game again until the 1970 World Cup, which was held in Mexico. In that game, they played Brazil. Like Italy, Brazil had won two previous championships. That meant that both teams were battling for a record-setting third World Cup title. Unfortunately for the Azzurri, the Brazilians were led by the greatest player in the history of soccer, the famous Pelé. Italy could

do little to stop Pelé and his talented team-mates. The Brazilians won, 4–1.

The 1982 tournament was held in Spain, and some experts thought that the Italians had a weak team. But the Azzurri proved their doubters wrong. Their star was Paolo Rossi, and in one game during the tournament, Rossi scored all of Italy's goals in a 3–2 win over Brazil. And in the championship against West Germany, he scored the first goal of the game and led his team to a 3–1 victory.

In 1990, Italy had won the honor of hosting the World Cup championship rounds. By then, Italy and Brazil had each won three World Cup championships, and millions of Italian fans expected the Azzurri to set a record with its fourth title. They were sadly disappointed. In the semifinal game, the Italians were defeated by Argentina, led by superstar Diego Maradona. It was a big disappointment for the Azzurri and their fans.

But in the 1994 World Cup, Italy was led by star player Roberto Baggio, who was famous both for his ponytail and his great offensive skills. Baggio and Italy made it all the way to the championship game, where they faced Brazil, the other three-time World Cup champion. The game was a close battle and incredibly tense.

Soccer Riots

When thousands of people get together in one place, they sometimes get out of control. Their behavior can get wild and violent, and at sporting events, this kind of atmosphere sometimes leads to riots. Riots are big, uncontrollable fights or stampedes involving many people.

For many years, soccer teams from Italy have had an intense rivalry with teams from England. On several occasions, the hard feelings between Italian and British fans have led to riots. The worst outbreak came on May 30, 1985, when a team from Turin, Italy, played a team from Liverpool, England, in the final of the European Cup. The Cup is a tournament held each year to determine the best team on the continent of Europe. The 1985 match was held in Brussels, the capital city of Belgium.

An estimated 10,000 Italian fans came to the game, along with about 20,000 fans from England. English fans are notorious for their violent actions at soccer events — and Italian fans are often the innocent victims. But this time, the Italian spectators shared the guilt. During the game, Italian and British fans started hurling insults at each other. Eventually the British fans rushed into an area where the Italians were sitting, which led quickly to a huge riot. As more people crowded to the scene of the riot, a big wall collapsed, killing 38 people and injuring almost 400 others.

After the final horn sounded, not a single goal had been scored. A 30-minute overtime period produced no goals, and the score was still tied at 0–0. That meant the game would be decided by a series of penalty kicks. In a penalty kick, an offensive player on one team tries to kick the ball past the other team's goalkeeper. Because the kicks are from close range, the offensive player usually has a big advantage over the goalkeeper. But not in this case. Baggio and team captain Franco Baresi both missed their penalty kicks. The Brazilians won with three successful penalty kicks to two for the Italians

Italy remains one of the elite soccer nations in the world, even though Brazil won their 1994 World Cup showdown. Will the Azzurri get revenge? One thing is for sure: It gives Italian fans something to cheer for.

Italy's Roberto Baggio is one of the most famous soccer stars in the world.

27

Chapter Three

Off to the Races

As we have already seen, the ancient Romans were obsessed with chariot racing. So perhaps it's not surprising that modern Italians adore races of many kinds. From the fiery roar of race cars to the whizzing wheels of a bicycle, Italian sports fans love cheering for anything that moves extremely fast.

The popularity of **auto racing** in Italy is not surprising. Italians love cars. The streets of big cities such as Rome are packed with noisy automobiles. In fact, statistics show that of all Europeans, Italians spend the most time in their cars. More than 2,000 years before there was any such thing as a car, the Italians had already invented roads. In the days before the ancient Roman Empire, people traveled from place to place along trails or paths. When it rained, these paths got so wet and muddy that neither humans nor horses could navigate them.

A stretch of the Via Appia that still exists in present-day Italy

The Romans solved this problem by inventing paved roadways. The first and most famous of those roads, the Via Appia, was begun in 312 B.C. In the next several hundred years, the Romans completed 53,000 miles (85,295 km) of paved roads. Italians also played an important role in the development of the automobile. In 1889, for example, Giuseppe Pirelli made the first tires designed especially for automobiles. Italians also built the first modern highway for cars. Inaugurated in 1924, this road was called the Autostrada.

Ever since the earliest days of the automobile, Italians have been wild about car races. In 1907, a big race was held from Peking, China, to Paris, France — halfway across the world! A team of three Italians, including a nobleman named Prince Borghese, won the race. It took them 60 days to get from Peking to Paris, and they beat their nearest competitors by almost three weeks.

One little boy who undoubtedly heard of that race was named Enzo Ferrari. Enzo was born in the city of Modena, Italy, in 1898. When he was growing up, he often went to auto races. He loved to see the cars speed around the track and wanted to be a racer himself one day.

Enzo Ferrari in one of his 1924 automobiles

In 1920, Enzo got his chance. He was hired as race driver for the famous Italian car company Alfa Romeo. The experience was a real thrill for Enzo. He decided that someday, he would open his own car company. Eventually, he did just that. By the time Enzo died in 1988, the Ferrari company was one of the most famous car manufacturers in the world.

Today, Italian fans take great national pride in race cars made by the Ferrari company. The company became famous manufacturing cars

The modern Ferrari company produces some of the fastest race cars in the world.

driven in Grand Prix auto races. These races —
also known as Formula One events — are the
most prestigious of the sport. Two Grand Prix
auto races are held in Italy. One is the Italian
Grand Prix, held at the famous Monza racecourse in the northern city of Milan. The other
is the San Marino Grand Prix, held at the city
of Imola, just a few miles from the Ferrari headquarters at Maranello. At both of these races,
the stands are packed with thousands of
screaming Italian fans, who wear scarlet-colored
Ferrari caps and wave flags adorned with a
picture of a prancing horse, the symbol of the
famous auto company.

The start of the Italian Grand Prix (top) and the race's jubilant
winners (right)

Italy's Mario Andretti won the prestigious Indianapolis 500 in 1969. After winning the race, burn scars were visible above his mouth due to a fiery crash during practice.

Mario Andretti was born in the Italian town of Montona in 1940. When he was only 13 years old, he began racing cars against other Italian boys. Two years later, the Andretti family moved to the United States and settled in Nazareth, Pennsylvania. In his new country, Mario continued racing and eventually became a professional. In 1965, he finished third in the Indianapolis 500. That was a great accomplishment because the Indy 500 is the most famous race in the United States. Every year, about 300,000 people go to the race — the largest crowd at any sports event in the country.

In 1969, Mario won the Indy 500. But that was just the start. He went on to have one of the most successful and durable careers in the history of the sport. Mario finally retired in 1994, but the Andretti name lives on. Now his sons, Michael and John, are top professional drivers!

About a century ago, a man named Eduardo Bianchi attached a motor to one of his bicycles, creating the first Italian motorcyle. Ever since that time, Italians have been fascinated with motorcycles and **motorcycle racing**. Several important races are held in Italy each year. And over the decades, Italian companies such as Moto Guzzi, MV Augusta, Gilera, and Ducati have gained worldwide fame for building excellent racing cycles. Some Italians have also become top riders. One of the most famous Italian motorcyclists of the 1960s and 1970s was Giacomo Agostini. The handsome Giacomo was so popular among Italian fans that movie companies asked him to act in their films.

Giacomo Agostini

35

Leonardo da Vinci and the Bicycle

Leonardo da Vinci (right) was one of the world's greatest artists. He was born in 1452, during a period of amazing artistic and scientific progress known as the Renaissance. Da Vinci painted many beautiful pictures, such as the famous *Mona Lisa*. In addition, Leonardo was a brilliant architect, scientist, and inventor. For example, he came up with the basic idea for the airplane hundreds of years before it was actually built.

Some people also believe that Leonardo was the first person to think of the bicycle. In the notebooks where Leonardo recorded his ideas, there's a sketch of a vehicle that looks very much like the modern bicycle (right). Historians think the drawing was made in about 1493 — more than 300 years before the bicycle was actually invented. Some experts, however, believe that one of Leonardo's assistants made the drawing.

Italians are known as some of the most knowledgeable and intense **bicycle racing** fans anywhere. Every year, Italy is home to a huge bicycle race known as the Giro d'Italia, which means "Tour of Italy." The Giro spans several weeks in May and June. The racecourse is spread out all over Italy. By the end of the race, competitors have cycled for a total of about 2,500 miles (4,023 km). The Giro is held on regular streets and roads, but Italy also has two of the world's most famous tracks

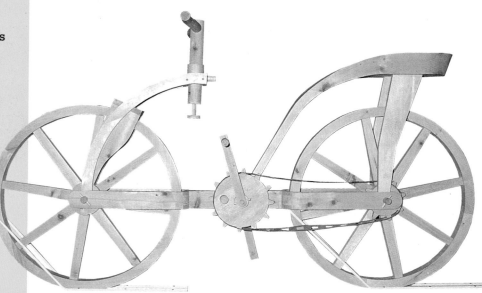

36

built especially for bicycle races. One is the Vigorelli Velodrome in Milan. The other is a track built in Rome for the 1960 Olympic Games.

The Giro is the second most important bike race in the world behind the Tour of France. One legendary champion of both races was Fausto Coppi, who lived from 1918 until 1960. While growing up in Italy, Fausto became interested in biking when he worked as a delivery boy at a butcher shop. He went on to become the top cyclist of the world during the 1940s, winning the Giro five times and the Tour of France twice.

A steep, winding stretch of the Giro d'Italia (top)
Fausto Coppi (right)

How Do I Race?

A lot of people think that riding a bike is easy. But for professional cyclists, such as those who compete in the Giro d'Italia, bicycle riding is incredibly difficult. To get an idea of what it's like to compete in the Giro, try a simple experiment:

1. Find an exercise bicycle that has an odometer. An odometer is a special device that keeps track of how far a vehicle such as a bike or car has traveled. If your parents don't have an exercise bike, you might be able to find one at school or at a nearby recreation center.

2. Ask an adult to help you adjust the seat of the exercise bike to fit your legs, and how to reset the odometer to zero.

3. Begin to cycle. Pedal as fast and as hard as you can. Try to pedal for 1 mile (1.6 km).

Are you out of breath? You should be. Pedaling fast for a whole mile is a lot of work. But now think about this. In the Giro d'Italia, cyclists have to pedal fast for about 2,500 miles (4,023 km). And they often have to ride up huge mountains! Now you can understand why bike racers are some of the most skillful and highly trained athletes in the world.

Bicycle racing is more popular
in Italy than it is in perhaps
any other country.

The annual palio festival in Siena, Italy, dates back many centuries.

Every summer in the Italian city of Siena, an event takes place that might seem strange to an outsider. On two days of the year, July 2 and August 16, thousands of people gather in the square at the center of the town. As trumpeters and drummers play, the excitement builds. And suddenly, it's time for a **horse race** to begin. Ten horses and their riders jolt into action. These riders have no saddles, so every now and then one of them gets thrown off his horse. The horses and their riders dash around the square three times — an event that takes about two minutes. The first rider to cross the finish line is swarmed by hundreds of fans as a huge celebration party begins.

This race is called a *palio*, which is the Italian word for "banner." It has its origins in the Middle Ages, when knights in armor would race against each other. The winner of those races was awarded the victory banner. And today — even though armor is no longer used — the palio is still given to the winning rider.

Residents of Siena aren't the only Italians with a historic love of horse races. In Rome, for example, nobles of the Middle Ages also raced against each other in the streets. But as the years passed, the city became too crowded for these wild events. So in the 19th century, the races were moved to a piece of land in the nearby countryside. Today, that site is the home of Le Capannelle, the city's horse-racing track. Since 1884, the country's most noted professional race, the Italian Derby, has been held at Le Capannelle.

A Venice gondolier

The city of Venice, located in northeastern Italy on the Adriatic Sea, is one of the most beautiful and unusual places on earth. The city is built on more than a hundred little islands. These islands are separated by thin strips of water called canals. For many centuries, people from Venice have used these canals to get from one part of the city to another by traveling on long, thin boats called gondolas. The drivers of these boats, known as gondoliers, take people around Venice on the canals — just like taxi drivers do on the streets of other cities.

In their spare time, the gondoliers also like to have **boat races** against each other. The most important of these competitions is called the Regata Storica, which means "historical boat race." This race dates all the way back to at least A.D. 1300. No one knows quite how the competition got started, but some people say it began when pirates kidnapped some women from Venice and tried to escape by boat. According to this legend, the local gondoliers chased after the pirates and killed them. The race may have come from the celebrations marking this event.

The Regata Storica in Venice (above & opposite page, bottom) is one of the most colorful and historical sporting events in the world.

Today, the Regata Storica is held on the first Sunday of September at the Grand Canal, the largest and most famous waterway in Venice. The day begins with a big parade of beautiful old-fashioned boats. Then comes the race. As thousands of spectators cheer from the banks of the canal, boats rowed by teams of professional gondoliers speed down the course. Members of the winning teams get big prizes. But even more importantly, they become heroes all over Venice. Losers are left to dream of next year's Regata Storica.

Chapter Four

Other Competitive Sports

Basketball is Italy's most popular spectator sport after soccer. This game was invented in the United States in 1891, but today basketball fever has infected much of Europe and the Middle East. One of basketball's first entries into Europe came during World War I, when Italian military officers asked the YMCA to teach basketball to their soldiers. After the war, basketball started gaining popularity throughout Italy.

Today, Italy has its own professional basketball league that draws more than two million fans to its games a year. Italian League games are also watched closely by scouts for National Basketball Association (NBA) teams in North America. Several current NBA players, including Toni Kukoc, Dino Radja, Brian Shaw, and Danny Ferry, played in the Italian League during their careers. But despite basketball's popularity in Italy, it has a long way to go before it replaces soccer as the number-one sport. In fact, five times as many Italians play soccer as play basketball.

Team Italy begins an international basketball game with a jump ball.

45

Italy's volleyball team is one of the best in the world.

Another American-invented game that has a large following in Italy is **volleyball**. Like basketball, volleyball was invented in the United States in the late 1890s, and it also caught on in Italy after World War I. Today the country has the best professional volleyball league in the world. Many of the finest players have competed in the Italian league, including the great American player Karch Kiraly.

Perhaps the reason volleyball is so well liked in Italy is that Italian sports fans love fast-paced

Italy's men's team celebrates after winning the 1994 world championship of volleyball.

sports. The tifosi get a thrill out of watching the ball fly back and forth across the net, as players dive and roll across the floor in an effort to return their opponents' shots. Italy's national volleyball teams are considered to be among the best in the world. In 1990 and 1994, for example, the men's team won the volleyball world championship, which is held once every four years. Italian kids love volleyball, too, and many of them play in special leagues organized for young people.

Italian skiing hero Alberto Tomba is lifted to his teammates' shoulders after winning an Olympic medal.

Northern Italy has some of the most beautiful mountains in the world. These snow-capped peaks are part of the Alps, the largest mountain chain in Europe. Thousands of Italians visit the Alps each year to take part in one of the nation's more popular sports, skiing. For most Italians, skiing is only a hobby. But Italy is also home to some of the world's best competitive skiers.

In the 1988 Winter Olympics for example, an Italian named Alberto Tomba won gold medals in both the giant slalom and slalom events — competitions in which he had to ski as fast as he could downhill on a zigzag course. Then, in 1992, Tomba set an Olympic record when he won the men's giant slalom competition for the second straight time. That same year, he finished second in the slalom event. In so doing, he became the first man in history to win a total of four medals in Olympic downhill skiing events. Italian women have also distinguished themselves in skiing competitions. In the 1994 Olympics, for example, Deborah Compagnoni won the gold medal in the giant slalom event.

Italian skiing champ Deborah Compagnoni

Fencing is a sport that involves sword fighting. But it's not at all like the swordplay you see in movies. In the first place, the competitors are not trying to hurt each other. They wear protective gear, and their weapons are specially designed to minimize injury. The object of fencing is to touch your opponent with your weapon, without allowing your opponent to touch you.

Fencing is an ancient sport, but Italians have played an important role in its development. The first book on fencing, published in 1536, was written by an Italian named Achille

Marozzo. In the 18th century, one of the most famous fencing masters was Domenico Angelo, who also wrote a popular book on the sport. Great 19th-century Italian fencers included the famous Giuseppe Radaelli. Today Italian fencers are still among the best in the world, with both men's and women's teams consistently doing well in the Olympics and the world championships.

Italy has been a fencing power for centuries.

PREUSS SCHOOL

51

Chapter Five

Italian Games and Other Leisure Activities

Bocce is a favorite Italian pastime. It is a kind of bowling game originally played in the Italian Alps about 2,000 years ago. In those days, people played bocce with stones. But today they use balls and play on special courts that can be found in parks all over Italy. Bocce can be played with two or four players. To start the game, a ball called a *pallino* is tossed underhand onto the court. The object of bocce is to toss your ball closer to the pallino than your opposition does. It's a pretty simple game—and maybe that's why it has remained so popular for all these years.

Bocce (left) is a favorite Italian pastime, as are skiing and mountain hiking in the Italian Alps (opposite page).

How Do I Play Bocce?

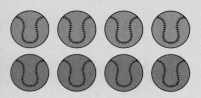

Bocce Equipment

Four colored baseballs (bocce balls) for each team

One golf ball (pallino)

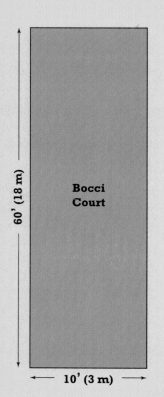

Bocci Court

60' (18 m)

10' (3 m)

If you don't live in Europe, it's unlikely that there is a bocce court near you. Also, bocce balls are difficult to find in most countries. But it is possible to gain a basic understanding of how the game is played by using substitute items. If you have three other players, here's how you can get started:

1. On a lawn or a grass playground area, mark out a court area that is 10 feet (3 meters) wide and 60 feet (18 m) long. You might do this by pushing sticks into the ground at the corners of the court, then running a piece of string around all four sticks.

2. Get one golf ball and eight baseballs. Four of the baseballs should be a different color than the other ones. If you can't get different colored baseballs, draw an "X" on four of the balls so that you can tell them apart from the others.

3. Split into two teams of two players each. Each team uses a different color of baseball.

4. Standing at one end of the bocce court, one of the players throws the golf ball underhand down the court. The golf ball is a substitute for the pallino.

54

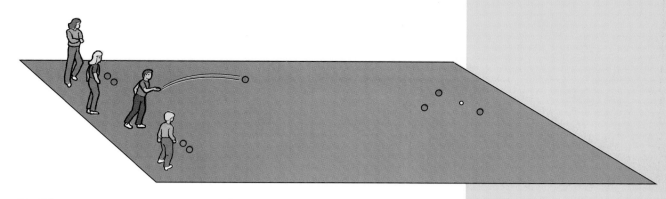

5. The two teams now take turns tossing their baseballs underhand in an effort to get closest to the pallino. It's OK if they knock their opponents' balls or the golf ball. If a ball rolls off the court, it is out of play, but if the golf ball rolls out, it is placed at a predesignated spot in the middle of the far end of the court.

6. After all the baseballs are thrown, count up the score. A team gets one point for each of its balls that are nearer to the pallino than the opposition's closest ball.

7. A game ends when a team reaches 12 points, but you must win by 2 points. If the score is tied at 11, the teams keep playing more rounds until one team is ahead by 2 points. The first team to win two out of three games wins the match.

Italians love **card games**. It's not unusual to see children playing cards in the street or old men playing at tables outside of taverns. Italy's fascination with cards goes back many centuries. One of the most famous type of cards was invented in Italy around 1430. These cards, known for their beautiful pictures, were called *tarocchi,* but today they are commonly known as *tarot* cards. Italians still play card games such as *scarto* with tarot cards. But these cards also have another use. Some people claim that they can tell fortunes using tarot cards!

Italians also use the standard playing cards with kings, queens, and jacks. Italian games using these cards are *scopa* and *scopone,* which are somewhat similar to the popular children's card game Go Fish. Italians also love to play bridge, and are considered excellent players. In fact, between 1957 and 1969, the Italian bridge team won the world championship in every year but one.

Some Italians believe that tarot cards (above) can tell one's fortune. Italians are also fond of many other types of card games.

56

Rheinhold Messner

Because northern Italy is home to the majestic Alps, many Italians like to spend their vacations **hiking** in the mountains. Italy also has some of the most popular peaks for mountain climbers — including the famous Matterhorn, which is nearly 15,000 feet (4,572 m) tall. Not surprisingly, several important mountain climbers have been Italian. In 1988 Italian Rheinhold Messner climbed the tallest peak in the world, Asia's Mount Everest, which is more than 29,000 feet (8,839 m) high. And he did it all by himself! To this day, he remains the only person to have climbed Mount Everest without companions, but several other mountaineers have died trying.

The Italian Alps

The 5,300-Year-Old Hiker

Sometimes, a recreational hike can lead to historic discoveries. In September 1991, a German couple was hiking high in the Italian Alps. As they walked near a huge field of ice and snow known as a glacier, they saw the head of a dead man sticking up out of the ice. At first, everybody thought the man was a hiker or skier who had died recently. But when authorities took the body to a laboratory for investigation, they made an amazing discovery. The body was 5,300 years old!

Scientists now believe that the man lived in the Stone Age, a thousand years before the Egyptians built the pyramids. He died during a hike through the mountains, and his body was immediately covered with snow. Because it never gets very warm in the mountains, the snow didn't melt for more than 5,000 years. And because the body was frozen, it was almost perfectly preserved. The ice also preserved much of the man's tools and clothes, including parts of an ancient backpack. Scientists say that the "Iceman" is as close as we'll come to meeting a real person from the Stone Age.

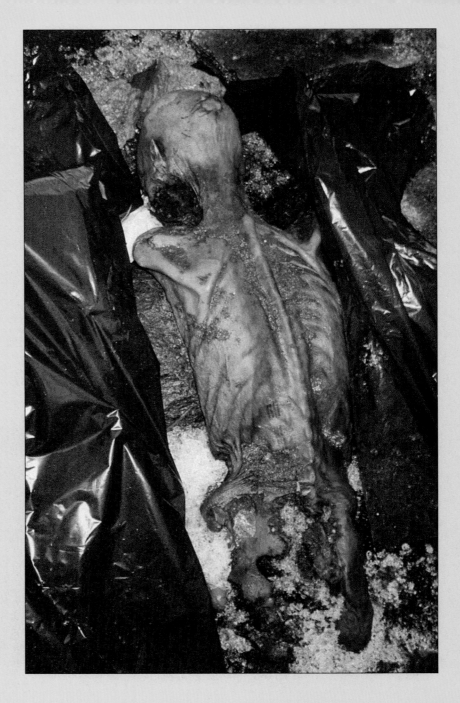

Italy is surrounded almost entirely by water. It also has some beautiful lakes, including the famous Lake Como. So it's no wonder that **sailing** is a favorite leisure activity of Italians. In fact, sailing has a very important role in Italy's economy, history, and folklore.

But the Italian love of sailing has also had a big impact on the rest of the world. The story of one Italian sailor is particularly important. The sailor was born in 1451 in Genoa, a port city on the Mediterranean Sea in northern Italy. Like a lot of boys in Genoa, he loved the

sea — and when he grew up, he began to work in ships. In 1476, a boat he was in was wrecked off the coast of Portugal, but he was able to find his way ashore. He kept sailing. As he got older, he dreamed of visiting far-off places. In 1492, he got his big chance.

Does this story sound familiar? It should. The man's name was Cristoforo Colombo, but we know him better as Christopher Columbus!

lossary

amphitheater
a large theater or stadium

Azzurri
Italian term meaning "the Blues," the name of the Italian national soccer team

bocce
a lawn-bowling game that is popular in Italy

chariot races
popular sport in ancient Rome in which men raced in horse-drawn carts (chariots)

charioteer
a driver of a chariot in a chariot race

Circus Maximus
the biggest stadium in ancient Rome used for chariot races

Colosseum
the largest amphitheater in ancient Rome; its ruins still stand in Rome today

fascism
system of government that is the opposite of a democracy — individual citizens have few rights and are controlled completely by the government

Ferrari
famous Italian automobile manufacturer, founded by Enzo Ferrari in the 1920s

football
the term used in most countries for "soccer" (which is the term used mostly in the United States)

Forza Italia
sports slogan meaning "Go, Italy!" that was also used in a political campaign by Italian prime minister Silvio Berlusconi

Giro d'Italia
"Tour of Italy"; a famous bicycle race that takes racers around Italy over the span of several weeks

gladiators
men in ancient Rome who fought to the death for sport

gondola
Italian term for the boats used to transport people through the canals in the city of Venice

gondolier
a person who pilots
a gondola

harpastum
ancient game similar to
modern soccer

Middle Ages
a period in European history
(approximately A.D. 400 –
1400) from the end of the
Roman Empire to the beginning of the Renaissance

palio
Italian term meaning
"banner"; also the name
of a historic horse race that
takes place every year in
the city of Siena

pallino
small white ball used in bocce

Regata Storica
"historical boat race"; an
annual gondola race in
Venice that has taken place
for centuries

Renaissance
a period of creativi-
ty and growth in
Europe that spanned
from about the 14th to the
16th centuries A.D.

Roman Empire
powerful civilization founded
in 753 B.C. by Romulus and
Remus

tifosi
Italian term referring to
dedicated sports fans

Via Appia
the "Appian Way"; a road
built by ancient Romans
beginning in 312 B.C. that
eventually connected
Rome with Capua

velodrome
an oval-shaped
racecourse built
specifically for
bicycle racing

World Cup
the international soccer tournament held every four years
in which national teams from
many countries compete
against each other

YMCA
Young Men's Christian
Association; an organization
begun in the 1850s that pro-
vides athletic and educational
services to its members

61

For Further Information

Books

Buckland, Simon. **Guide to Italy**. Kingfisher, 1994.

Corbishley, Mike. **Everyday Life in Roman Times**. Franklin Watts, 1994.

Howard, Dale. **Soccer Around the World**. Children's Press, 1994.

Mariella, Cinzia. **Passport to Italy**. Franklin Watts, 1994.

Stein, R. Conrad. **Italy**. Children's Press, 1984.

Wright, Nicola. **Getting to Know Italy & Italian**. Barron, 1993.

Online Sites

The Bocce Site
http://www.ultranet.com/%7Ejfrat/bocce.html
Bocce rules, schedules, discussion, etc.

Formula One Grand Prix
http:www.shell-ferrari.com/netcatch/9P107.html
Race schedules, information on drivers, etc.

In Italy Online
http://www.initaly.com/initaly/
Webzine written by Americans living in Italy

The Roberto Baggio Super Fans Home Page
http://www.island.net%7Edsanders.rbhp.html
Website for fans of the Italian soccer player

The Italian Soccer Connection
http:www.vol.it/RETE_/14/1da.html
Running commentary on soccer action in the Italian League

World Cup History
http://www.wmart.com/soccer.WC94.hist.html
Detailed history of World Cup soccer

The World of Juventus
http://fbox.vt.edu:10021/M/mmakonne/juve/juve.html
Website devoted to the Italian soccer team Juventus

Index

Photo Credits

Cover, ©Elio Castoira; 1 (top left), ©Giorgio Benvenuti/Olympia/PhotoEdit; 1 (top right), ©Rick Stewart/AllSport; 1 (bottom), Photri; 2–3, ©Phil Cantor/SuperStock; 4, ©Paolo Nucci/Olympia/PhotoEdit; 5, ©Chris Cole/AllSport; 6, Corbis-Bettmann; 7 (top), AP/Wide World; 7 (bottom), UPI/Corbis-Bettmann; 10, ©Blumebild/H. Armstrong Roberts; 11, SuperStock; 12, Archive Photos; 13, Photri; 14, 15, Corbis-Bettmann; 16, ©R. Matassa/H. Armstrong Roberts; 17, Photri; 18, ©S. Siro/Olympia/PhotoEdit; 19, ©Rick Stewart/AllSport; 20, ©Robert Fried; 21, ©Claudio Villa/AllSport; 22, Allsport; 23 (left), Photri; 23 (right), Olympia/PhotoEdit; 24, ©Cesare Galimberti/Olympia/PhotoEdit; 26, Reuters/Corbis-Bettmann; 27, ©Focus on Sports; 28, ©Pascal Rondeau/AllSport; 29, 30, SuperStock; 31, UPI/Corbis-Bettmann; 32, ©Charles Oricco/SuperStock; 33 (top), ©Camerique/H. Armstrong Roberts; 33 (bottom), ©Anton Want/AllSport; 34 (top), UPI/Corbis-Bettmann; 34 (bottom), ©Mitchell B. Reibel/Sports Photo Masters, Inc.; 35 (both photos), Olympia/PhotoEdit; 36 (top), SuperStock; 36 (bottom), 37 (top), Olympia/PhotoEdit; 37 (bottom), AP/Wide World; 39, Olympia/PhotoEdit; 40 (left), Archive Photos; 40 (right), UPI/Corbis-Bettmann; 41, ©Robert Fried; 42 (top), ©Steve Vidler/SuperStock; 42 (bottom), SuperStock; 43, ©ZEFA/H. Armstrong Roberts; 44, Olympia/PhotoEdit; 45, ©David Klutho/AllSport; 46, 47, ©La Monaca/Olympia/PhotoEdit; 48, ©Aldo Martinuzzi/Olympia/PhotoEdit; 49, ©Giorgio Benvenuti/Olympia/PhotoEdit; 50, ©Phil Cantor/SuperStock; 51, ©Scott Barrow/SuperStock; 52, 53, SuperStock; 56, ©Roy King/SuperStock; 57 (top), Reuter/Corbis-Bettmann; 57 (bottom), H. Armstrong Roberts; 58, 59, Olympis/PhotoEdit

About the Author

Miles Harvey is a journalist who has written for many national publications. He is the author of many books for Children's Press, including biographies of Deion Sanders, Barry Bonds, Juan Gonzalez, and Hakeem Olajuwon, as well as the Cornerstones of Freedom titles *The Fall of the Soviet Union, Presidential Elections,* and *Women's Voting Rights.* He lives in Chicago with his wife, Rengin.